The Quiz Book for BFFs 2

by H. Becker

Scholastic Canada Ltd.
Toronto New York London Auckland Sydney
Mexico City New Delhi Hong Kong Buenos Aires

Scholastic Canada Ltd.
604 King Street West, Toronto, Ontario M5V 1E1, Canada

Scholastic Inc.
557 Broadway, New York, NY 10012, USA

Scholastic Australia Pty Limited
PO Box 579, Gosford, NSW 2250, Australia

Scholastic New Zealand Limited
Private Bag 94407, Botany, Manukau 2163, New Zealand

Scholastic Children's Books
Euston House, 24 Eversholt Street, London NW1 1DB, UK

www.scholastic.ca

Library and Archives Canada Cataloguing in Publication

Becker, Helaine, 1961-, author
The quiz book for BFFs 2 / by H. Becker.

ISBN 978-1-4431-2879-7 (pbk.)

1. Best friends--Juvenile literature. 2. Children's questions
and answers. I. Title.

HQ784.F7B43 2014   j302.34083   C2013-907812-6

6 5 4 3 2 1   Printed in Canada   121   14 15 16 17 18

Table of Contents

Are You Destined to Remain Friends?

Using the chart below, add up the number value of the letters of your name. If the sum is two or more digits long — for example, 23 — add those numbers together (2 + 3 = 5) to get a single digit. You may need to do this again to get a single digit. This final one-digit figure is your magic number.

A=1	I=9	Q=17	Y=25
B=2	J=10	R=18	Z=26
C=3	K=11	S=19	
D=4	L=12	T=20	
E=5	M=13	U=21	
D=6	N=14	V=22	
G=7	O=15	W=23	
H=8	P=16	X=24	

Now find the magic number for your BFF. Add her number to your number to come up with a single value. Reduce the number to a single digit as above if necessary.

This is your friendship factor. It reveals the future of your friendship.

4

What your friendship factor means . . .

1 Your friendship is rock solid. It can't be broken apart by anyone or anything. You've *won* the lottery with this BFF!

2 Your friendship is pure magic.
Like a pair of shoes or peanut butter and jelly, you work better together than apart. You complement each other, like blue and orange. This friendship is *too* strong to be divided!

3 Is there another friend in your inner circle? Of course there is! You've got so much love in your hearts it feels only natural to let other gals in. Sharing the fun doubles (or triples!) it.

4 A square has four straight sides. That makes it one of the most stable geometric shapes. Your friendship is just as stable. Don't forget to occasionally think outside of the box — throwing a curve into your time together will keep this friendship rocking and rolling!

5 High-five! This is the number of competition and victory. That sums up your friendship too. Sometimes you're up, sometimes you're down. Sometimes you fight, sometimes you're an unbeatable team! But in the end, you always figure out how to make your friendship a winner.

6 You have so much in common! You think alike, act alike, even like the same clothes and music! But you don't always connect on a deeper level. Are you on parallel paths that never really meet?

7 Lucky number seven says your friendship is blessed by good fortune and a lifetime of fun. But don't take this friendship for granted. Luck can turn. It takes effort to make even the most favoured friendships last. Beware of gossip. Jealous acquaintances can tear you apart.

8 Crazy eight defines your friendship. And your friendship is crazy all right! What do you two see in each other? You're as different as chalk and cheese, bologna and scissors! But that's what makes it work — that you bring different talents and tastes to the table. Somehow, this glorious, kooky friendship rises above your differences. Savour it, though, because this wacky style of friendship doesn't always last. That doesn't mean it isn't a blast while you're in it.

9 Is your friendship infinite, like the circle at the top of the number nine? Or does it have a sharp, short end, like number nine's tail? No one knows for sure. Your friendship is a mystery. It works according to its own inner logic and follows its own rules. Will it last or wither? Only time will tell.

How Well Do You Know Your BFF?

Quiz A

Answer each of the following questions about your friend.
Have her answer the same questions about you to find out your BFF IQ.

What does she prefer?

1. Autumn or spring?
2. Sun or moon?
3. Unicorns or trolls?
4. Furry or silky?
5. New York or Paris?
6. Golden eagle or dove?
7. Tag or dodge ball?
8. Wolverine or Iron Man?
9. Curling or bowling?
10. Snowman or snow angel?

11. Candy corn or licorice?

12. Scrapbooking or beading?

13. 50 metre dash or 5K run?

14. Morning person or night owl?

15. Truth or dare?

Scoring

Find out which answers were right and give each other a point for each one. Your combined score tells you your BFF IQ.

How you rate . . .

0-5 Go ahead — introduce yourselves to each other.

6-12 Delightfully different — and terrific together!

13-24 Can you read each other's you-know-what?

25-30 Perfect partners in crime!

So You Think You Can Dance?

You don't have to be a disco diva to enjoy burning up the dance floor or to create your own signature dance with your BFF.

Grab your BFF and choose your fave tune. Start with some of these popular dance moves by following the diagrams. Then add your own personal flair for a sizzlin' routine that's yours and yours alone.

1. **The Grapevine.** This deliciously easy dance step will have you winding your way around the dance floor in no time. Mix with a few other dance steps for extra punch. Then throw in some funky hand motions and shoulder shimmies. You'll have stirred up a juicy routine all your own!

   Each "step" has a number on it. The number indicates the order in which you move each foot. 1) Move your right foot one step to the right. 2) Cross your left foot behind your right foot. 3) Right foot again! 4) Left foot again! Bring it next to your right foot to complete one "grapevine." Continue in the same direction (until you run out of room), then switch feet and direction to groove your grapevine to the left.

2. **The Mambo.** Mambo is THE classic Latin dance step — the foundation of salsa and many other fiesta faves. You'll be cooking with hot sauce when you show off this hot-n-spicy dance style.

Do this series of steps facing each other so that one partner is mirroring the other's steps. Or mix it up with other steps (like The Grapevine) for show-stopping sizzle.

1) Move your left foot forward. 2) Shift your weight to the back foot. 3) Move your left foot back. 4) Pause with your feet together. 5) Move your right foot back. 6) Shift your weight to the front foot. 7) Move your right foot forward. 8) Pause with your feet together. Then go back to step 1 and start all over.

3. **The Square Dance Do-si-do.** Do this dance step facing each other with your arms crossed and held out in front of you. Circle around each other, passing each other on the right (so your right shoulders almost touch). Keep your body facing the same direction in which you started.

Start

4. **Square Dance Swing Your Partner.** Face each other. Link your right elbows and spin in a circle. Switch to link your left elbows. Spin in a circle in the opposite direction. Repeat as many times as desired.

5. **The Cancan.** Stand next to each other and do each step in unison.

1) Jump in place, lifting your left knee. 2) Land with both feet together, then kick your left toe in front of you as high as you can. 3) Land feet together, then jump in place, lifting your right knee. 4) Land feet together, then kick your right toe in front of you as high as you can. Repeat as many times as desired.

6. **The Macarena.** This party fave is extra fun when you do each step in unison with your peeps. To learn it, stand beside your BFF facing the mirror. Do each move first on the right side then on the left, holding for two beats on each side. Count the step numbers out loud and see if you can match each other's motions perfectly. Then do them in time with your music! Invent your own dance by substituting steps of your own for a few of these.

1) Extend right arm out in front of you, palm down, then the left. 2) Turn right palm up, then the left. 3) Cross your right arm over your chest, then the left. 4) Bring your right hand to the back of your neck or head, then the left. 5) Bring your right hand to your left hip, then your left hand to your right hip. 6) Bring your right hand to your behind, then the left. 7) Swivel time! Bend your knees and rock your hips: left, right, left. 8) Jump and turn ¼ turn to the right. Repeat from step 1 as many times as you like!

Will Your Friendship Last?

Answer yes or no to each of the following questions.

1. My friend and I are both blabbermouths — we can't keep secrets!
2. My friend and I share so many interests!
3. My friend has a selfish streak — she tends to put herself first.
4. I worry that my friend could turn on me.
5. My friend always knows the exact right thing to say to make me feel good about myself.
6. My friend is always nice, even when she's in a bad mood.
7. I get so jealous of my friend sometimes.
8. My friend always asks for my advice, or to solve her problems for her.
9. My friend is 100 percent reliable — the kind of person I would trust to feed my fish when I'm on vacation.
10. My friend and I have one big thing in common. But other than that, we're as different as can be.

Scoring

1	Yes 0	No 10
2.	Yes 10	No 5
3.	Yes 0	No 10
4.	Yes 0	No 5
5.	Yes 10	No 0
6.	Yes 10	No 0
7.	Yes 0	No 10
8.	Yes 0	No 5
9.	Yes 10	No 0
10.	Yes 0	No 10

How you rate . . .

5-30 Enjoy the moment. Some friendships are for the long haul. Some are just for fun, just for now. You two may move on and go your own ways in the future, but that doesn't mean what you share now isn't special and wonderful.

35-55 Stick to it. Keeping a friendship strong requires plenty of work, and plenty of patience and understanding. You two have the basics — trust, caring and fun. Add a little elbow grease and this friendship might be one you will share for years to come.

60-90 Stuck like glue. There's so much good stuff between you — laughter, support, honesty, adventure. You encourage each other to be the best you each can be, and truly celebrate one another's successes. That's the recipe for staying best friends forever. Give yourself a pat on the back, and then give one to your BFF!

What Are Your Brains Made Of?

What's on your mind? What's on your BFF's? Divide up the brain pictured here like a pie chart and mark what your brains are (mostly) made of! Here are some categories to consider. Add your own as needed!

- Clothes
- School work
- Pizza
- Video games
- World peace
- Boys
- Social life
- Lunch
- Toe jam
- Conspiracy theories
- Kittens
- Planning a slumber party
- Friendship quizzes
- Zombies
- Music

Meh or Eek?

Read over the items listed below. Are they ho hum *checks fingernails, yawns* or do they send you running into the hills screaming? Answer Meh or Eek! for each item to get your scare score. Compare your scare score with your BFF's and see who's the bigger scaredy cat!

1. A slug slithering across your bare skin.
2. Spiders. Big, hairy spiders.
3. A rabid dog.
4. Giving a speech.
5. Camping. Bears.
6. Heights.
7. The haunted house on the hill.
8. An unidentified ooze rising in your basement.
9. Hornets. Hundreds of hornets.
10. The zombie apocalypse.
11. An alien invasion.
12. Rats.
13. Being trapped in a very small, dark space.
14. Swimming in shark-infested waters.

15. Walking through a cemetery at night.
16. Piles and piles of French homework.
17. Bungee!
18. Leeches. The kind that can crawl out of the water to track down a meal.
19. Taking a test you haven't studied for.
20. A vampire in your bedroom, about to feast on your throat.

Scoring
Give yourself one point for each EEK!

How you rate . . .
0-5 Ice runs through your veins.
6-10 Cool as a cucumber.
11-14 Nervous Nellie.
15-20 Scaredy cat.

Which Trailblazer Is She?

Answer the following questions about your pal. Find out which famous trailblazer she most resembles and why!

1. What motivates your BFF most?
    a. Fame or power. > Go to question 2.
    b. Adventure. > Go to question 3.
    c. Curiosity. > Go to question 4.
    d. Justice. > Go to question 9.
2. Which describes your BFF best?
    a. A bit of a diva. > Go to question 6.
    b. Determined and hard working. > Go to question 7.
3. Your BFF is more . . .
    a. science-oriented. > Go to question 11.
    b. artsy. > Go to question 5.
4. Which does your BFF prefer?
    a. Nature. > Go to question 8.
    b. Numbers. > Go to question 11.
5. Your BFF prefers . . .
    a. country life. > She is EMILY CARR.
    b. social life. > She is LUCY MAUD MONTGOMERY.

6. Which sounds more like your BFF?
   a. Fashion first. > She is COCO CHANEL.
   b. Exploring new territory. > Go to question 10.
   c. Fashion AND power, dahling. > Go to question 12.
7. Your BFF is more . . .
   a. sporty. > She is HAYLEY WICKENHEISER.
   b. literary. > She is LUCY MAUD MONTGOMERY.

8. Which would your BFF prefer?
   a. Working with people. > Go to question 9.
   b. Working with aliens. > She is ROBERTA BONDAR.
   c. Working with animals. > She is JANE GOODALL.
9. Would your BFF rather . . .
   a. be in the thick of the action? > She is HARRIET TUBMAN.
   b. be the go-between, the communicator extraordinaire? >
   She is NELLIE MCCLUNG.
10. Is your BFF more . . .
    a. adventurous? > She is TAQULITTUQ.
    b. caring? > She is JENNY TROUT.
11. What does your BFF prefer?
    a. Video games. > She is GRACE HOPPER.
    b. Puzzles. > She is HYPATIA.
12. Which country would your BFF prefer to visit?
    a. Egypt. > She is CLEOPATRA.
    b. China. > She is WU ZETIAN.

What your BFF's trailblazer persona means . . .

Roberta Bondar is Canada's first female astronaut. If your BFF is like Roberta Bondar, she is not afraid of new experiences. She likes to live "on the edge" and is often considered a leader. She knows how to be a team player, too, and people like her. A lot.

Emily Carr was a Canadian artist whose distinctive painting style has made her a Canadian icon. If your BFF is like Emily Carr, she is an innovator and ahead of her time. She may have to overcome many obstacles to make her dreams come true, but a true visionary like her will always find success.

Coco Chanel was an influential fashion designer who created the modern fashion business. If your BFF is like Coco Chanel, she has exquisite style and a flawless fashion sense. She loves fashion magazines, fashion shows and fashion trends. She'd like nothing more than to be a fashion designer herself!

Cleopatra was the last pharaoh of Egypt and a famous diplomat, strategist and romantic heroine. If your BFF is like Cleopatra, she can literally rule the world. She has hidden strengths and a superb ability to read people and make them like her. She is also a very responsible caregiver and would make a great babysitter!

Jane Goodall is a British primate expert who has spent 45 years studying chimpanzees in Africa. If your BFF is like Jane Goodall, she has a deep love of animals and people and a serious concern about the environment. She possesses great strength of character and a focused approach to life that will lead her to success.

Grace Hopper was an American computer scientist and United States navy rear admiral. Her work led to the development of COBOL, one of the first modern programming languages. If your BFF is like Grace Hopper, she is good at math and science and has a very logical mind. She likes solving problems and creating new things. She is very tidy and orderly!

Hypatia was an ancient Greek philosopher, mathematician and the first female astronomer. She was also the head of the famous School of Alexandria, where she taught the greatest intellectuals of the day. If your BFF is like Hypatia, she is a terrific teacher, with a sharp mind and an intuitive understanding for how to inspire others. She also knows how to wear a toga.

Nellie McClung was a Canadian feminist, politician and social activist. She was instrumental in passing the laws that gave women in Canada the right to vote. If your BFF is like Nellie McClung, she is totally girl power! She will fight for what she believes is right and won't let anyone stand in her way.

Lucy Maud Montgomery was a Canadian novelist whose *Anne of Green Gables* book series is one of the best-loved stories of all time. If your BFF is like Lucy Maud Montgomery, she is creative and funny with a mischievous streak. She is ambitious but is not really comfortable with the limelight and would prefer to observe from the sidelines. She is very loyal to her friends and has incredible perseverance.

Taqulittuq was an Inuk guide and explorer who assisted European explorers in the Arctic and whose Northern hunting skills kept them alive in treacherous conditions. If your BFF is like Taqulittuq, she is wise, courageous and loves to travel. She is very interested in people and in learning new things. She is the first to try new foods and new fashions. She's a great storyteller too!

Jenny Trout was the first woman to be licensed to practise medicine in Canada. If your BFF is like Jenny Trout, she has a sincere desire to help others. She is a logical thinker and very hands-on — a doer rather than a talker. She has so much energy!

Harriet Tubman was an American abolitionist who was one of the leading "conductors" on the Underground Railroad. She personally led more than 300 American slaves to freedom in Canada. If your BFF is like Harriet Tubman, she is daring, clever and brave. She cares deeply about other people and wants to help make the world better for everyone. She also knows her own mind and is not easily influenced by others.

Hayley Wickenheiser is the first woman to play full-time professional hockey in a position other than goalie. As a member of the Canadian women's national ice hockey team, she won four Olympic gold medals and one silver and was twice named tournament MVP. She is widely considered the world's greatest female hockey player. If your BFF is like Hayley Wickenheiser, she is strong, smart and versatile. She can do anything she puts her mind to!

Wu Zetian was the only female Chinese emperor. Her reign was one of the most peaceful and culturally diverse periods in Chinese history. If your BFF is like Wu Zetian, she is definitely a leader! She is always exciting to be around, but has a terrible temper. She is very trustworthy and loyal to people who deserve it.

Would You Rather . . . ?

Which would you choose? Which would your BFF? Compare your answers to see how alike you are.

Would you rather . . .

1. get stuck without shoes or without toilet paper?
2. get a sunburn or frostbite?
3. spend one day in a viper pit or one night in a haunted house?
4. be sick with a horrible stomach ache or look after a friend with a horrible stomach ache?
5. not be able to read or not be able to write?
6. get trapped in a closet or accidentally locked out of the house?
7. eat bacon-flavoured ice cream or super spicy "suicide" chicken wings?
8. live without friends or live without money?
9. go hungry for a day or eat a fried mealworm?
10. have a week with tons of homework or a week with no homework but a big test on Friday?
11. get lice or athlete's foot?
12. go a day without talking or a day without food?

13. hold a poisonous scorpion or be chased by a ravenous tiger?
14. have more siblings or no siblings?
15. see into the future or be able to read minds?
16. face a horde of killer ants or a swarm of killer bees?
17. use a pogo stick on ice or a snowboard on slush?
18. be in the path of a tsunami or a lava eruption?
19. spend the rest of your life indoors or the rest of your life outdoors?
20. be seasick or lovesick?

Scoring

Give yourself a point for each answer you had in common.

How you rate . . .

0-6 Rather be anywhere . . . but taking this quiz!
7-14 Rather similar . . . but you agree to disagree.
15-20 Rather freaky . . . how much you think alike!

Fill-in-the-Blanks Funny Story

Read the story out loud. Fill in the blanks according to the instructions as you read. Don't forget to let your best friend have a turn reading it to you!

_____ woke up one morning feeling ill.
    \<your BFF's name>

She threw off the covers. Her feet were _____.
                                            \<adjective>

Her skin was _____. She had turned into
                \<adjective>

a _____!
    \<animal>

She got out of bed and _____ into the kitchen.
                        \<verb ending in ed>

Her family saw her and they _____.
                                \<animal noise ending in ed>

" _____!" they shouted. "You look
      \<your BFF>

_____!"
 \<how your favourite food tastes>

"Thank you," she said. Then she _____.
                                \<verb ending in ed>

At school, all the kids _____ at her.
                         \<verb ending in ed>

They couldn't believe she had turned into a _____.
                                \<same animal>

29

Suddenly she was the most _____ kid in school!

<adjective>

During art class she was able to paint the most beautiful painting with her _____.

<animal body part>

During phys. ed. she was the star at _____.

<sport>

In the cafeteria, she surprised everyone when she ate with her _____. That's when _____

<body part>　　　　　　　　　　　　　<your principal>

came in. _____ was sooooo _____ !

<your BFF>　　　　　　　　　<a feeling>

The principal said, " _____ !"

<something a doctor says>

So _____ went home, crawling on her

<your BFF>

_____.

<body part>

She got into bed and _____ herself to sleep.

<verb ending in ed>

When she woke the next morning, she looked down and was happy to see she was no longer a _____.

<same animal>

But when she went to brush her teeth, she got another shock. Her nose had become a _____ !

<vegetable>

30

Do You See
What I See?

Study this blob. Do you see an animal? Does your BFF?

Scoring

This activity is based on a famous test used in psychology experiments. It's called a Rorschach test, and is used to assess people's personalities and emotional states.

What your answers reveal about your BFF and you . . .

If you both chose YES . . .

• you and your BFF are quite normal. No — really. You are.

If you both chose NO . . .

• Whoa! Are you sure you two are human? Or were your fathers androids and your mothers wildebeests? Do you each have six legs, perhaps? You two are so off-the-charts peculiar that the FBI has your faces on a poster that reads: Wanted — Identification of this species.

If one of you chose YES and the other chose NO . . .

• you need to keep a careful eye on one another. SHE might turn into a cat before your very eyes. SHE might steal your socks. You know who we mean.

How Well Do You Know Your BFF?

Quiz B

Answer each of the following questions about your friend, then have her answer the same questions about you.

Which does your BFF prefer?

1. Hoodie or cardigan?
2. T-shirt or turtleneck?
3. Mini-skirt or yoga pants?
4. Brights or black?
5. Beret or baseball cap?
6. Trendy or classic?
7. Wild prints or sedate solids?
8. Mix or match?
9. Tights or knee highs?
10. Heels or flats?
11. Bracelets or earrings?
12. Headband or ponytail?
13. Scarf or belt?
14. Classic or glam?
15. Vest or pullover?

Scoring

Add up your combined score — the total number of right answers — to find out your BFF IQ.

How you rate . . .

0-5 Mix 'n' match. Your tastes in clothing may differ, but you agree your friendship is beautiful!

6-12 Sisters in stylin'. Your friendship will never go out of style.

13-24 Totally coordinated! Your friendship is ahead of the trend.

25-30 Matching outfits! You're perfectly paired, in all ways!

Princess, Peasant or Jester?

So which of you is queen of the castle? And who's the dirty rascal? Take this quiz separately and then compare your answers to find out if you're a royal, a serf or just plain silly.

1. Would you rather . . .
    a. clean a toilet?
    b. clean a diamond — a radioactive one?
    c. clean up a zoo enclosure?
2. Which would you rather have?
    a. A ticket to a Broadway show.
    b. A ticket to an NHL game.
    c. A ticket to a comics convention.

3. Who would you rather meet?
    a. Justin Bieber.
    b. Princess Kate.
    c. Tigger.
4. Where would you rather live?
    a. Disney World.
    b. Monte Carlo.
    c. A cabin in the woods.

5. How would you describe your pajamas?
   a. Pretty in pink.
   b. Practical.
   c. Printed with pictures of sushi.
6. Supper time! You're serving . . .
   a. burgers and fries.
   b. sloppy Joes.
   c. caviar.

7. At school people consider you . . .
   a. a brain.
   b. a pain.
   c. insane.
8. Recess! What do you like to play?
   a. Four square.
   b. Tag.
   c. Monkey bar tag.
9. Which animal do you like the best?
   a. Kittens are sooo cute!
   b. Puppies are soooo cute!
   c. Wildebeests are soooo cute!
10. Which is your favourite flower?
    a. Snapdragons.
    b. Roses.
    c. Tulips.

Scoring

1. a1   b5   c10
2. a5   b1   c10
3. a1   b5   c10
4. a10   b5   c1
5. a5   b1   c10
6. a1   b10   c5
7. a5   b1   c10
8. a5   b1   c10
9. a5   b1   c10
10. a10 b5   c1

How you rate . . .

10-49 Peasant. You're just an ordinary gal and proud of it!

50-70 Princess. Naturally you're royalty, dahling!

70+ Get yourself the jester's cap. You're clown to the court!

The Kookiest Contest (For BFFs Only!)

There's nothing like a little friendly competition — especially when the contest ends up with two winners! Try the activities below. Decide together how you'll score whose efforts are "best" or "funniest."

1. Who can do jumping jacks longer?
2. Who can cross her eyes best?
3. Who can stand on her head longer?
4. Who can do the most somersaults in a row?
5. Who can do the most push ups?
6. Who can throw a bean bag the farthest?
7. Who can write her name neatest?
8. Who can draw the best elephant?

9. Who can make the funniest sound?
10. Who can sing the highest note?
11. Who is the most "double jointed"?
12. Who can skip rope "hot pepper" the greatest number of times without missing?
13. Who can scream the loudest?
14. Who can crack the most knuckles/joints?
15. Who can make the best monkey face?

What Sports Star Is She?

Being a sports superstar is not just about athletic talent. It's also about grit, determination and style. Which sports hero is most like your BFF? Take this quiz to find out!

1. What is your BFF more likely to say?
   a. I have a need for speed. > Go to question 2.
   b. Slow and steady wins the race. > Go to question 3.
2. Your BFF is highly self-motivated.
   a. True. > Go to question 4.
   b. False. > Go to question 5.
3. Your BFF is happiest working . . .
   a. alone. > Go to question 6.
   b. in a group. > Go to question 7.
4. Which term best describes your BFF?
   a. Focused. > She is CHARMAINE CROOKS, five-time Olympian in track and field.
   b. Versatile. > She is CLARA HUGHES, Olympic cyclist AND speed skater.
5. Your BFF would prefer . . .
   a. a road trip. > She is DANICA PATRICK, NASCAR race car driver.
   b. a sailing trip. > She is SILKEN LAUMANN, Olympic rower.

6.   Which shape best represents your BFF?
     a. A straight line. > She is MARIA SHARAPOVA, tennis star
     and the world's highest-paid female athlete.
     b. A circle. > She is YUNA KIM, the 2010 Olympic figure
     skating champion.

7.   Is your BFF more like . . .
     a. summer? > She is CHRISTINE SINCLAIR, captain of the
     Canadian women's national soccer team.
     b. winter? > She is MARIE-PHILIP POULIN of the Canadian
     women's national hockey team.

Who she is . . .

Charmaine Crooks. She's in the running for nicest person and
bestest BFF ever! She has lots of determination. No hurdle is too
high for her and she will overcome anything that stands in her
way. No one would ever call her a half-miler!

Clara Hughes. Talk about versatile! Your BFF is good at
everything! She's got a sharp mind, too, and really knows how to
roll with the punches.

Yuna Kim. She can figure out how to solve any problem, whether it's a math question or what-to-wear crisis. With her upbeat attitude and winning smile, she makes everything look easy, but she's a hard worker. She also knows how to spin a story.

Silken Laumann. She's a smooth talker with lots of charm. But she can be sensitive at times and is easily hurt. Nothing gets her down for long, though — she thinks life is but a dream.

Danica Patrick. This gal has plenty of drive and ambition. When she puts the pedal to the metal, she leaves everyone else in the dust! But if she's not careful, she can run out of gas. Remind her to take some chill time to recharge her batteries.

Marie-Philip Poulin. She's one cool customer — unflappable in a crisis and focused on her goals. She has terrific "stick-to-it-iveness" and never gives up!

Maria Sharapova. When your BFF walks into a room, people notice. They love her and want to pay court to her! But she doesn't let it go to her head. She keeps her eye on the ball. She is also very open-minded.

Christine Sinclair. Hanging with your BFF is always such a kick. She knows how to have fun — give her a great idea and she'll run with it. She's a team player and a popular and effective leader.

42

Choose Her New Hair Style

How will your best bud look with a new do? Help her choose what look she'll like!

1. She prefers . . .
   a. easy care. > Go to question 2.
   b. glam. > Go to question 5.
   c. funky. > Go to question 10.
   d. fun. > Go to question 12.
   e. everyone else's hair but her own. > Go to question 17.

2. Is she into sports?
   a. Yes. > Go to question 3.
   b. No. > Go to question 4.

3. Does she like to change her style now and then, or is one look good to go?
   a. Change is good. > She should try the fun DOUBLE BUN!
   b. One look is good. > She should try SHORT AND SASSY!

4. Are her locks curly or straight?
   a. Curly. > Let it grow to MID-SHOULDER LENGTH for extra versatility.
   b. Straight. > Go for the CLASSIC PONY!
   c. Somewhere in between. > Go to question 7.

5. Is her style sleek or sassy?
   a. Sleek. > Go to question 6.
   b. Sassy. > Go to question 9.

6. Is her hair long or short?

    a. Long. > Go to question 7.

    b. Short. > SIDE PART WITH GEL is the go-to do!

7. Cut it, or keep it long?

    a. Get out the scissors! > Go to question 8.

    b. She'd never agree to a cut. > Try a FRENCH BRAID then!

8. Fashion forward or more of a classic type?

    a. Fashion forward. > ASYMMETRICAL is the cut for her!

    b. Classic. > A CHIN-LENGTH BOB is her go-to do.

9. Is she a girly girl?

    a. Not at all. > Give her SPIKES WITH GEL!

    b. Sort of. > Leave it LONG AND FLOWY!

    c. Definitely. > Go to question 16.

10. Is she more artsy or more mathy?

    a. Artsy. > Go to question 11.

    b. Mathy. > Go to question 12.

11. Does she prefer dance or theatre?

    a. Dance. > A BALLERINA BUN is the prima choice!

    b. Theatre. > Go for big drama with wash-out HOT PINK DYE.

12. Is her hair curly, wavy or straight?

    a. Curly. > Go to question 13.

    b. Wavy. > Go to question 14.

    c. Straight. > Go to question 15.

13. Does she like to be the centre of attention?

    a. No way! > Let it grow LONG, LONGER, LONGEST!

    b. You bet. > TWO POOFY PONYTAILS that look like Teddy Bear ears are super fun!

14. Is her hair longer or shorter?

    a. Longer. > LOTS AND LOTS OF LITTLE BRAIDS are swingy fun for long-haired gals.

    b. Shorter. > Make a zingy LIGHTNING BOLT PART and twist small sections of hair with multicoloured hair bands for flashy fun.

15. Is her hair thicker or thinner?

    a. Thick and a little coarse. > A SINGLE LONG BRAID at the back.

    b. Thick and shiny. > Cut super short into a FUNKY BRUSH CUT.

    c. Thin and silky. > Shoulder length with BANGS is just the ticket!

16. Does she prefer shiny things or soft, cuddly things?

    a. Shiny things. > Add fabulous jewelled hair pins and a cute TIARA!

    b. Soft, cuddly things. > Secure a LOW PONYTAIL with a huge velvet bow.

17. What would she like to change about her hair?

    a. Its colour. > Go to question 18.

    b. It's too curly. > Get out the flat iron, then try a HALF PONYTAIL style.

    c. It's too thin. > Get out the curling iron. A WAVY BOB is the answer.

    d. It just hangs there. > Go to question 19.

18. Does she want lighter colour, darker colour or different colour?

    a.   Lighter colour. > Try a LEMON JUICE RINSE for an all natural Goldilocks look.

    b.   Darker or redder. > Try a HENNA rinse for a more exotic, French fashion.

    c.   Different! > Go big or go home with PURPLE STREAKS!

19. Will she cut it?

    a.   Definitely. > Go to question 20.

    b.   Nope. > Go for an UPDO with some pretty or funky accessories, like combs and scrunchies, to add flair.

20. How short?

    a.   Chin length. > SIDE PART and let it SWING!

    b.   Super short! > SHAVE one side and let the top and back go all TOUSLED.

What each hair style says about your BFF . . .

Asymmetrical cut. She's an independent, original thinker. And kooky — just a little kooky.

Ballerina bun. She keeps everyone on their toes.

Bangs. She's sharp — a Powerpuff girl with bang-on style!

Chin-length bob. She enjoys sledding and is up for adventure!

Classic ponytail. She loves animals, especially sea horses and rocking horses. She enjoys vigorous activities like sports, mountain climbing and eating corn on the cob. She loves country and western music and just horsing around with her friends.

Double bun. She loves pastry. Sometimes she gets hot and cross, but she's always sweet at heart.

French braid. She has a very twisted sense of humour.

Funky brush cut. She's a no-nonsense gal and will win at the sweepstakes of life.

Half ponytail. She is cautious and doesn't like to jump into things. She thinks the cup is half full.

Henna. No one ever called your brave pal chicken!

Hot pink dye. She's a trendsetter (or an Irish setter — they both have great colour hair!) and always cooler than cool!

Lemon juice rinse. Do blondes have more fun? If they are all like your BFF, they do. How do you bear it?

Lightning bolt part. Of course she's bright. She frequently changes her mind. She has a very sparkly personality.

Long and flowy. She's a true romantic and she adores her BFF!

Long, longer, longest! She isn't afraid to do things her own way, or to tell others they should do them her way too!

Lots and lots of little braids. She's good at all kinds of crafts, especially weaving and basket making.

Low ponytail. She is a hopeless romantic. She sighs every time she sees a big-eyed puppy or a kitten.

And unicorns! Oooh! She loves unicorns. She'd like nothing better than to wake up one morning in a historical novel like *Anne of Green Gables* or *Black Beauty*. She has beautiful handwriting.

Mid-shoulder length. This gal can fit in everywhere and adapt to new situations easily. Don't give her the cold shoulder!

Purple streaks. Can you say woo-hoo! This gal is a one-woman fun machine.

Shaved and tousled. With her lively and quirky personality, your BFF can make even bedhead look good.

Short and sassy. She's quick — good at math, at sports and setting the table. She can do anything she sets her mind to.

Side part and swingy. She's playful and imaginative. She enjoys going to parks.

Side part with gel. She's very serious minded and determined to succeed. Will she? Of course!

Single long braid. She's a bit old-fashioned — loyal, trustworthy and sensitive. No wonder you've chosen her as your BFF!

Spikes with gel. Expect fireworks when this gal comes around! She's got strong opinions and isn't afraid to speak her mind.

Tiara. Diamonds are a girl's best friend, aren't they? And doesn't your BFF deserve them? Of course she does — she's warm, kind and wonderful!

Two poofy ponytails. She loves to make others laugh. Why shouldn't they enjoy life as much as she does?

Wavy bob. She has many moods, from classic to kooky. No wonder she's so exciting to be around! She's also an excellent swimmer.

Updo. She combines timeless elegance with a modern outlook. She knows how to make the best of a bad situation and turn life into a ball.

Twins Separated at Birth?

Do you love the same things and think the same way, or are you and your BFF living proof that opposites attract? To find out, pick 1 (for dislike or disagree), 2 (for meh . . .) or 3 (for love or agree) for each item. Have your BFF do the same.

1. Trilobites
2. Frozen yogurt
3. I am an excellent gymnast.
4. Vanilla-bacon cupcakes
5. Playing hangman
6. Lady Gaga
7. I'm an athlete.
8. Sunglasses
9. The Hunger Games
10. Funky barrettes
11. Skulls
12. Stuffed animals
13. I love to do experiments!
14. Romantic comedies
15. Hamsters
16. Skateboarding
17. Playing card games
18. I have a sensitive nose.
19. The smell of popcorn
20. Boys are silly.
21. Sci-fi movies
22. Purple stripes in your hair

23. Building snow forts
24. Dangly charms on bracelets
25. Adventure video games
26. I'm a thoughtful person.
27. Pancakes for dinner
28. I prefer being cold to being hot.
29. Chili peppers
30. I enjoy my own company and don't mind being alone.
31. Dolphins
32. Playing football
33. Santa hats
34. Stargazing
35. Tobogganing
36. Anything cooking-related
37. Jewellery-making
38. Borscht
39. Skirts
40. Herring
41. Neon
42. I want to be a writer when I grow up.
43. Puzzles
44. Fishing
45. I can't sleep in an unmade bed.
46. T-shirts with cartoon characters on them
47. Making movies
48. I'd like a chinchilla as a pet.
49. I love math.
50. Square dancing

Scoring

Add up your total of answers that match. Double the total number — if you have 12 matching answers, for example, give yourself a score of 24 (12 + 12 = 24).

How you rate . . .

90-100 Identical twins. Definitely! You are so similar you might as well be clones.

50-89 Fraternal twins. You share so much in common, no wonder you're BFFs!

20-49 Soul sisters, maybe. Your differences complement each other; in fact, they're what make your friendship so strong!

0-19 Third cousins, once removed. You agree on one thing and one thing only: you love, love, love hanging out together!

Drawn Together

Do you two think alike? Do you *draw* alike?

Below are some partially completed illustrations. Copy them twice, on two separate pieces of paper, one for you and one for your BFF. Then complete each picture. How similar are your finished pictures? How different are they? Whose are most realistic? Most colourful? WACKIEST?

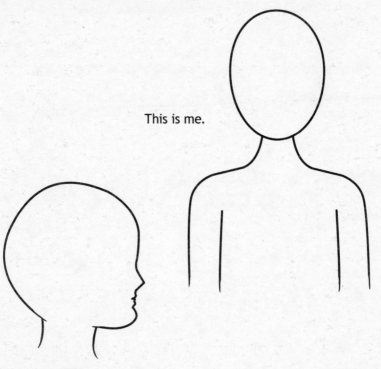

This is me.

This is my BFF.

Werewolf, Vampire or Zombie?

So you're both far from normal. Everybody knows that. But are you truly monstrous? And if so, what kind of monster are you? And what is your BFF? Take this horrible quiz to discover the terrible truth.

1. In the morning, you . . .
   a. take it slow but steady.
   b. are up and at 'em!
   c. are *so* not a morning person — you're reaching for that snooze button!
2. Which frightens you the most?
   a. A zit. A really, really ugly zit.
   b. A bad hair day.
   c. A fashion fiasco.

3. Choose a nail polish shade.
   a. Apple Red.
   b. Black Tornado.
   c. Lime-ade.
4. Which sport appeals to you most?
   a. Hang gliding.
   b. Ultra marathon.
   c. Touch football, in the mud.
5. You have an art project to finish. What will you make?
   a. Something out of clay.
   b. Something sparkly.
   c. Something soft and fuzzy.

6. Which would you rather do?
    a. A crossword puzzle.
    b. Play Frisbee.
    c. Dance.

7. Choose a hat.
    a. Ball cap.
    b. Tuque.
    c. Wide brimmed, glamour girl sun hat.
8. Do you sleep with a stuffed toy?
    a. No.
    b. Yes, and it's old and falling apart.
    c. Yes, and it's a soft, fluffy animal.
9. Which would be your fantasy pet?
    a. A giant pink gerbil.
    b. A komodo dragon.
    c. A unicorn.
10. Which is your fantasy vacay?
    a. Paris, dahling.
    b. A cabin in the woods.
    c. Ahhh, spa . . .

Scoring

1.	a5	b10	c20		6.	a20	b10	c5
2.	a5	b10	c20		7.	a5	b10	c20
3.	a10	b20	c5		8.	a20	b5	c10
4.	a20	b10	c5		9.	a20	b5	c10
5.	a5	b20	c10		10.	a20	b10	c5

How you rate . . .

50-95 Zombie. You care very little about what others think. You are very focused on your goals and not easily deterred from your path. You like to take things slow, and are not much of a talker, but you really know how to get your point across. Wash your hands more often.

100-150 Werewolf. You are very versatile. One day you're creative and focused, the next you're a whirlwind of activity. You love the great outdoors, animals and jewellery with the moon and stars on it. You have a sharp mind and a very slobbery tongue.

155-200 Vampire. No wonder your friends come to you for advice — you seem older and wiser than most people your age. But you can sometimes be aloof — cold even. And who can blame you? You can be hurt by the smallest things: a harsh word, a sharpened stake. You have a tremendous thirst for knowledge.

Is She a Yogi?
Are You?

Are you both human pretzels? Try these yoga moves to see if you're as flexible as a hair elastic or stiff as a new notebook.

1. **Cat-Cow** — Start by getting on all fours with your back flat. This is TABLE. Then arch your back, extending your neck and spine. This is COW. Round your back, rolling your shoulders toward your ears. This is CAT. Slowly alternate between CAT and COW to stretch your back. Ahhh . . . doesn't that feel great?

2. **Downward Dog** — From TABLE (see #1), straighten your legs, sending your seat bones as high as you can, and let your head drop between your arms. This is a terrific all-body stretch.

3. **Tree** — Stand with both feet together. Place the sole of one foot against your other leg, either above or below your knee (not on your knee). Hold your hands in front of you in the prayer position. Fix your eyes on a single point and balance on one foot for as long as you can. Then switch sides. This pose is great for balance and concentration.

4. **Happy Baby** — Lie on your back and grasp both feet as shown, letting your knees flop out to the sides. Gently let yourself roll back and forth. Doesn't that feel good?

5. **Child's Pose** — Finish your yoga practice with CHILD'S POSE. Kneel on the floor with your knees slightly apart. Fold forward at the waist and rest your forehead on the floor in front of you. Stretch your arms out in front of you. Feel the amazing stretch in your back and shoulders. Ahhh . . .

Visual Puzzler

Sometimes two heads are better than one. Can you and your BFF solve these tricky rebus puzzles together?

1 OVER OVER

2 M1Y L1I1F1E

3 PROMISE

4 REST
YOUR

5 YOUR TIME

6 SGEG

7 ge it it it it

8 search
and

9 Hi Way
Pass

10 P
O
U
R

63

Scoring . . .

Give yourself one point for each correct answer.

1. Over and over again
2. For once in my life
3. Broken promise
4. You're under arrest!
5. Your time is up!
6. Scrambled eggs
7. Go for it!
8. Search high and low
9. Highway overpass
10. Downpour

How you rate . . .

0-1 Still at the starting line. But together, you're bound to cross the finish line of fun!

2-4 You are big thinkers. And *big* winners at friendship too!

5-7 There's so much fun in your friendship. And you two clever kids are bound to find it.

8-10 You're on top of the world. You two can solve any problem together!

How Well Do You Know Your BFF?

Quiz C

Answer each of the following questions about your friend then have her answer the same questions about you.

What does she like best?

1. Eggs with ketchup or no ketchup?
2. Mild or extra spicy?
3. Meat-lover's pizza or extra cheese?
4. Sushi or ostrich meat?
5. Popcorn or tortilla chips?
6. Dark chocolate or milk chocolate?
7. Almond or coconut?
8. Oatmeal or puffed rice?
9. Milk or juice?
10. White bread or brown?
11. Tofu or turkey?
12. Stir fry or stew?
13. Cantaloupe or honeydew?
14. Salty or sweet?
15. Cake or pie?

Scoring

Find out which answers were right and give each other a point for each one. Your combined score tells you your BFF IQ.

How you rate . . .

0-5 Savoury. You bring exotic tastes to your friendship table. Savour your differences!

6-12 Spicy. Like a pepperoni pizza, your friendship delivers exciting flavours and experiences.

13-24 Chewy. There's a lot to sink your teeth into in this healthy relationship!

25-30 Sweeeeet. You go together like fudge + brownie.

Fill-in-the-Blanks Funny Story (The Next Chapter)

Read the story out loud. Fill in the blanks according to the instructions as you read. Don't forget to let your best friend have a turn reading it to you!

_____ and _____

        <your BFF's name>   <a boy you know>

went up the _____ to fetch a
                        <a piece of furniture>

pail of _____ .
            <something gross>

_____ fell down and broke his
        <the boy>

_____ . He started to
        <funny object>

_____ .
        <verb>

_____ went over to him and said,
        <your BFF>

"_____."
    <something they say over the P.A. at school>

_____ replied, "_____
    <the boy >   <something your mother says>

_____."

_____ got _____.
              <your BFF>   <an emotion>

She _____ and _____
        <verb ending in ed>   <another verb ending in ed>

him. Then she threw the pail of _____ on him.
                                <something gross>

"I never want to _____ you again!" she said.
                   <verb>

He said, " _____."
                <something you say to a pet>

So _____ went back down the
         <your BFF>

_____ , taking the pail with her. And
      <furniture>

nobody ever saw or heard from _____
                                <the boy >

ever again.

Best Friends
4 Evah Comic Strip

Your friendship is special so immortalize it in your own comic strip! Draw yourself and your BFF in each of the frames below. Don't forget to add funny voice balloons and sound effects (BLAM! GACK!) Here are some ideas to get your started . . .

What she looks like when she's ready for bed.

Here's what we look like doing our own invented dance routine.

This is what we each looked like as babies.

Here's what we'll each look like when we are grown up.

It was so hilarious when_____.

Oh no! BAD HAIR DAY!

Here's what_____would look like as a zombie.

In our best Halloween costumes.

Here's what we'd both look like if we were our favourite foods.

How we feel about dressing up in fancy clothes.

You're Sooo Weird!

Who's weirder, you or her? Take this very weird quiz separately and then compare your answers to find out!

1. Which is most fun?
   a. Eating worms — yum!
   b. Pretending to be a worm.
   c. Having a worm as a pet.

2. Which word best describes you?
   a. Interesting.
   b. Funny.
   c. Purple.

3. You swear there is WHAT living under your bed?
   a. Dust bunnies — and they're alive!
   b. Monsters, naturally.
   c. Cubic decilitres.

4. When you were a little kid . . .
   a. you thought your stuffed animals were alive.
   b. your favourite stuffed animal went on play dates with you.
   c. your favourite stuffed animal organized your play dates.

5. What colour are your fingernails?
   a. Depends on the day. Sometimes they are pink, sometimes black, sometimes they have no particular colour.
   b. Explain this word "fingernails."
   c. On our planet we do not have fingernails, we have tentacles.

6. If you were a tree . . .
   a. your bark would be worse than your bite.
   b. you'd drop seed pods on squirrels' heads just for fun.
   c. you'd like to be a Christmas tree.
7. Which kitchen tool is most like you?
   a. Knife, because you are sharp.
   b. Can opener, because you are helpful.
   c. Egg slicer, because you are an egg.
8. You are putting together a volleyball team for the school recess league. What team name do you suggest?
   a. The Volleywood Stars.
   b. The Cheese Steaks.
   c. The Volcano of Doom.
9. Which practical joke is the funniest?
   a. Fake vomit.
   b. The invisible dog on a leash.
   c. Arrow through the head.
10. Which fairy tale character do you most resemble?
    a. Rapunzel, because she's hairy.
    b. Cinderella, because she likes shoes.
    c. Rumpelstiltskin, because he knows his own name too!

Scoring

1. a5   b10 c1
2. a1   b5   c10
3. a5   b1   c10
4. a1   b5   c10
5. a1   b5   c10
6. a5   b10 c1
7. a5   b1   c10
8. a5   b1   c10
9. a1   b10 c5
10. a10 b5   c1

How you rate . . .

10-20 You are completely normal. Not weird at all. So not-weird, in fact, that you are actually somewhat peculiar.

21-40 You are just the right amount of weird.

41-70 You are weirdly weird. So weird, in fact, that most other people think you are just pretending to be weird. But we know better.

71+ You are off the charts weird. Run screaming to the hills weird. Your father is a lion and your mother smells like elderberries weird. Mad as a hatter, cuckoo as a clock, nutty as a peanut with a top hat and cane weird. The good news is there is a cure for your form of weirdness. The bad news is no one has discovered it yet.

WEIRD

What Type of Friend Are You?

Everybody has their own style of relating to others. Your temperament makes a difference when it comes to friendships too.

What's your friendship style?

1. You tend to have . . .
    a. just one or two close friends.
    b. four or five gal pals.
    c. lots and lots of friends — the more the merrier!
2. Your friendships tend to be . . .
    a. stormy.
    b. organized around common interests, like a sports team or fave activity.
    c. deep.
3. Which statement is most true of you?
    a. You find it easy to make new friends.
    b. Your friends change, it seems, with the seasons.
    c. You find it hard to make new friends.
4. Would you call yourself the jealous type?
    a. Yes.
    b. No.
5. How much do you share with your friends?
    a. Everything! They know everything about me and vice versa.
    b. Plenty — especially giggles and grins.
    c. Not that much — I prefer to keep my feelings to myself.

6. Do you worry a lot about what other people think of you?
    a. Yes! All the time.
    b. Sometimes.
    c. No. Why bother? They'll think what they want to think.
7. Would you describe yourself as very sensitive and easily hurt?
    a. Who, me? Naaaah.
    b. Sometimes.
    c. Definitely.
8. You've got to give a speech in front of a large group. Your BFF has offered to help you practise. What would you like her to do?
    a. Give me lots of reassurance and tell me I'm doing great!
    b. Help me correct my obvious mistakes, like when I'm talking too fast.
    c. Nothing. I'd prefer to practise on my own, in private.

Scoring

1. a1	b5	c10
2. a5	b10	c8
3. a15	b8	c1
4. a5	b10	
5. a5	b10	c15
6. a5	b10	c15
7. a15	b10	c5
8. a8	b12	c15

How you rate . . .

35-55 Shy. You find it difficult to break the ice with new people, but when you do, you are sensitive, loyal and generous. The upside: The friendships you make will be real, deep and long-lasting. Watch out for: Shying away. Give people a chance to know you by taking a risk and letting the real you show. You'll probably discover people are much more open and welcoming to you than you expect.

56-75 Intense. You care so deeply about people. Connecting with others can at times be exhausting and overwhelming. That's why you prefer to have one super-close friend rather than lots of so-so friends. Which can be great if you find that super-special BFF to bond with and not so great if you don't. The upside: You're bound to have fabulous friendships! Watch out for: The jealousy bug. Don't forget to leave your BFF room to breathe. She'll love you all the more for giving her some space.

76-98 Easy-pleasy. People like hanging with you because, well, you're fun and easy to get along with. Not a lot of drama. The upside: You're popular and enjoy lots of varied friendships. Watch out for: Over-extending yourself. You often find yourself pulled in several different directions, and you don't mean to let people down, but you're only one person! Try to be sensitive to other people's needs — they may not always be the same as your own.

99-105 Private. You might be the life of the party but find it tough to share your deepest feelings with others. The upside: You are very strong and self-reliant. You go, girl! Watch out for: Burnout. No one can take on the world alone. Friends are for tough times as well as party time. When you open up and share your troubles you'll find the load gets lighter and life looks brighter.

How Well Do You Understand Boys?

How well do you know boys? Take this quiz to find out. Then compare your score with your BFF to find out who's the boyo experto.

1. You have to choose a book for a boy in your class. You choose . . .
   a. a book chock full of sports facts.
   b. a superhero graphic novel.
   c. an adventure novel full of wizards and dragons.
2. You see three boys walking together down the street. You assume they are . . .
   a. on their way to the park to play football or another team sport.
   b. on their way to the movies to see an action-adventure flick.
   c. on their way to someone's house to play video games.
3. A boy in your class has just ignored you. That means . . .
   a. he likes you.
   b. he hates you.
   c. he has no idea who you are.
4. Which of these three activities would a boy rather do?
   a. Play laser tag.
   b. Practise archery.
   c. Have a water balloon fight.

5. When a boy says, "That was epic!" it means . . .
   a. he liked it.
   b. he hated it.
   c. he heard someone else say it.
6. Boys like . . .
   a. gross stuff.
   b. funny stuff.
   c. scary stuff.
7. You accidentally hit a boy in the head with a dodge ball. What will he do?
   a. Cry.
   b. Throw the ball right back at you!
   c. Pretend it didn't happen.
8. You are assigned a boy as your partner for a school project. You . . .
   a. let the boy decide who does what — they like to be in charge.
   b. do the project yourself — you can't count on boys to buckle down and do the work.
   c. split the work fairly and do your part — you know he'll do his just the way you'll do yours, and if not, that's his problem.

Scoring

Give yourself 0 points for each A answer. Give yourself 0 points for each B answer. Give yourself 0 points for each C answer.

How you rate . . .

0-0 What were you thinking? You are a girl! You will never understand boys. They are silly, silly creatures. No matter how hard you try, you will never be able to figure out why they think robotic monster cars are exciting or why they seem so clueless about all things essential like knowing people's names. Just shake your head and get on with the important business of running the world while they draw pictures of spaceships on their arms.

Extrovert, Introvert or Ambivert?

Are you Little Miss Outgoing? Or are you more the shy, retiring type? Answer YES or NO to find out whether you're a born extrovert (a person who is outgoing), introvert (a person who prefers their own company) or somewhere in the middle.

1. You like nothing better than a slumber party with lots of pals.
2. Too much noise wears you out.
3. The perfect day involves hanging out at home in your jammies.
4. You like quiet, on-your-own activities — reading, crafts, decorating your room.
5. You live for team sports.
6. Your favourite type of get-together is a sleepover with your bestie.
7. Your house is where all your pals gather — you love it when there's hustle and bustle!
8. You tell your best pals everything!
9. You're the one who makes social arrangements for your group of friends, making sure there's always something going on that you can do together.
10. You like to write in a journal or make drawings just for yourself.
11. Your favourite sports are ones you can do on your own, like swimming or running.
12. You feel most energized in a calm, quiet place.

13. You find it hard to focus when there are more than two or three people in the room.
14. Crowds — argh!!!
15. You're something of a performer — class clown, musician or chatterbox.

Scoring

1. yes 10 no 5
2. yes 5   no 10
3. yes 5   no 10
4. yes 5   no 10
5. yes 10 no 5
6. yes 5   no 10
7. yes 10 no 5
8. yes 10 no 5
9. yes 10 no 5
10. yes 5   no 10
11. yes 5   no 10
12. yes 5   no 10
13. yes 5   no 10
14. yes 5   no 10
15. yes 10 no 5

How you rate . . .

75-100 Introvert. An introvert is a person who gets her energy from within. Your batteries are charged up when you are on your own and depleted by large crowds, lots of noise and commotion. This doesn't mean you aren't social — it just means you need lots of alone time to keep yourself feeling balanced and happy. You prefer smaller get-togethers with close friends to huge, noisy bashes, and solitary, creative activities to team sports. Because you are self-directed, you tend to be an original thinker and are not easily distracted by bells and whistles. As a result, you can achieve great success in many different fields that require intense concentration, especially the arts, sciences and business.

105-120 Ambivert. Ambiverts are the most flexible personality type. You combine qualities of both your more outgoing friends and your more inward-looking ones, putting you in the "best of both worlds" category. You enjoy time on your own as much as you enjoy being "out there," and thrive on variety. Because you have qualities of both major personality types, you understand other people's feelings well. This makes you easy to get along with and a valued friend and colleague. Ambiverts do well in all fields, especially sales, education (you'd make a great teacher!) and collaborative fields like film-making or fashion.

125-150 Extrovert. An extrovert gets her energy from her interactions with other people. When you spend too much time alone, you get lethargic, bored and even depressed. You shine, though, when surrounded by people. You love to be where the action is, and when nothing's going on, you're the one to get things started! Extroverts are natural entertainers, entrepreneurs and politicians.

Two Heads Are Better Than One

Working together, can you and your BFF figure out these brain teasers?

1. What do you have to give before you can break it?
2. What goes up but never comes down?
3. What loses its head every morning, but gets it back again every night?
4. What has holes but can hold water?
5. What's as big as an elephant but weighs nothing?
6. What five-letter word becomes shorter when you add two letters to it?
7. Without it I'm dead. If I'm not, then I'm behind. What am I?
8. What can be cracked, made, told and played?
9. The more you take of me, the more you leave behind. What am I?
10. What has eyes but cannot see?
11. Mary's father has four children; three are named Nana, Nene and Nini. What is the fourth child's name?
12. It lives without a body, hears without ears, speaks without a mouth and is born in air. What is it?
13. What goes around and around the wood but never goes into the wood?
14. What do you break every time you name it?
15. What has four fingers and one thumb but is not alive?
16. How many letters are in the alphabet?
17. You can draw me, fire me or fill me in. What am I?

18. Where do you find roads without vehicles, forests without trees and cities without houses?
19. How many seconds are there in a year?
20. There's a one-storey house that's all yellow inside. The floor is yellow, the lamps are yellow, the walls are yellow — everything is yellow. So what colour are the interior stairs?

Scoring

Add up your combined score — the total number of right answers — to find out how you rate.

1. Your word.
2. Your age.
3. A pillow.
4. A sponge.
5. An elephant's shadow.
6. Short.
7. A head.
8. A joke.
9. Footsteps.
10. A potato.
11. Mary.
12. An echo.
13. The bark on a tree.
14. Silence.
15. A glove.
16. 11! Count them: "THE ALPHABET"
17. A blank.
18. On a map.
19. 12: January 2, February 2 . . . etc.
20. There are no stairs. The house is only one storey.

How you rate . . .

0-5 Riddle newbies. Luckily you're clever at choosing friends!

6-10 Sisters in solvin'. Your friendship is a smart idea!

11-14 Both brill! Great minds think alike!

15-20 Pure genius! You're a pair of prodigies and an A+ team!

Cat or Dog?

Are you a cat person or a dog person? What about your BFF? Take this quiz to find out whether your are purrfectly matched or doggone different!

1. Which would you prefer?
   a. Playing catch with a Frisbee.
   b. Snoozing on top of a radiator.
   c. Taking a walk in the woods.
2. Would you call yourself a people person?
   a. Yes. Definitely.
   b. Sometimes. I can be outgoing, but I also value alone time.
   c. Not so much. People consider me a very private person.
3. Which sport do you prefer?
   a. Yoga.
   b. Track and field.
   c. Fishing.
4. It's your birthday. What's your dream day?
   a. Spa, dahling.
   b. Hanging out at home.
   c. Rambling through a city with my bestie, taking in all the sights and sounds.
5. You're cooking dinner! What's on the menu?
   a. Barbecued salmon.
   b. Barbecued baby back ribs.
   c. Veggie pizza.

6. Your bestie has given you a new nickname. What is it?
   a. Scooby.
   b. Garfield.
   c. Cuddles McGee.
7. Is the glass half-empty or half-full?
   a. Half-full.
   b. Full, silly!
   c. Empty, but who cares as long as the glass is crystal!
8. Which do you prefer?
   a. Fries with catsup.
   b. Fries with gravy.
   c. Fries with vinegar.
9. You are buying a gift for your bestie. What will it be?
   a. A soccer ball.
   b. A fluffy stuffed animal.
   c. A can of tuna.

10. What animal drives you crazy?
   a. Evil mice. Definitely. Evil. Mice.
   b. Did someone say squirrel?
   c. That annoying bird that starts tweeting before dawn.

Scoring

1. a1 b3 c5	4. a5 b3 c1	7. a3 b1 c5	10. a5 b1 c3
2. a1 b3 c5	5. a5 b1 c3	8. a5 b1 c3	
3. a3 b1 c5	6. a1 b5 c3	9. a3 b1 c5	

10-22 100% Dog person. You are affectionate, eager to please and open-minded. You also have a tendency to slobber and jump up on people. But that doesn't stop them from loving you for your joyful enthusiasm, playful spirit and floppy ears. You are good at following instructions and an excellent team player.

23-36 Cat-dog combo. You are so lucky — a versatile person that combines the best quality of both dogs and cats in one special package! "Cogs" like you have beautiful hair and, naturally, superior grooming skills. You've got plenty of self-confidence and nothing gets you down.

37-50 100% Cat person. You are a rare breed — independent, brilliant and capable. You are definitely a leader, not a follower. Graceful, tidy and prone to hairballs, you win the admiration of all you meet. You bounce back from adversity — perhaps you really do have nine lives! Avoid people named Tweety or Jerry — they are out to get you.

What's Your EQ?

You've probably heard of IQ tests. They're supposed to measure intelligence. EQ tests measure emotional smarts — how good you are at recognizing and responding to emotions.

How well do you know your own feelings? What about your BFF's? Take this quiz to find out if you are emotionally aware or emotionally AWOL.

1. You usually hang out with the same group of gal pals. Do you always know exactly how each person in your clique feels about each other?

   a. Yes. I know all about who's tighter than tight and who are rivals.

   b. Sometimes. People's feelings can change awfully fast!

   c. Yes. We're all super good friends. Why else would we hang out together?

2. You woke up this morning feeling unsettled and unhappy. Do you know why?

   a. Must have woken up on the wrong side of the bed.

   b. Maybe because I had a bad dream?

   c. Yes. It was because of the argument I had with my sister before we went to sleep.

3. True or false: When you make a mistake, you get really down on yourself and become super self-critical.
   a. Totally.
   b. Sometimes.
   c. No way! Everyone makes mistakes now and then. Let it go.
4. You have to go see your teacher about your bad grade on an English test. How does this make you feel?
   a. Uncomfortable, but you take a deep breath and get it over with.
   b. Not great, but you know she will help you figure out how to improve your work, so it will work out in the end.
   c. Anxious and unhappy. You hate being put on the spot.
5. Do people call you a drama queen because you tend to overreact to little things?
   a. Nope.
   b. Sometimes.
   c. Omigod, that is soooo me!

6. Would you describe yourself as a good judge of character?

a. Yes. I can often tell if someone is truly kind and honest or if they are putting on an act.

b. Usually, although it surprises me when someone turns out to be more of a "frenemy" than a friend.

c. I always thought so, but lately I get confused by people who say one thing and do another.

7. You're arguing with your brother about whose turn it is to wash the dishes. Things are starting to get pretty heated and out of control. What do you do?

a. Suggest you both cool down a bit before making a decision.

b. Scream at him and call him names.

c. Just go ahead and do the dishes — even though you *know* it's his turn.

8. You have the chance to play on a Select hockey team. You know it will require a huge time commitment, and you're not sure if you are ready to do that. How will you make your decision?

a. Listen to your gut and follow your instincts.

b. Let your coach or your parents decide.

c. Make a list of pros and cons to help you decide.

9. Which statement best describes you?
   a. I make friends easily.
   b. I get along well with others, but I need plenty of time before I let others get close to me.
   c. I sometimes find it difficult to get to know other people.
10. Your bestie's pet died. She feels terrible. What do you do?
    a. Convince her to go out and have some fun to take her mind off Fluffy.
    b. Let her cry, and express your sympathy. Sometimes people just need to let their feelings out.
    c. Give her some time to herself. No one wants people around at a time like this, do they?

Scoring

1. a3   b2   c1
2. a1   b2   c3
3. a1   b2   c3
4. a3   b2   c1
5. a3   b2   c1
6. a3   b2   c1
7. a3   b1   c2
8. a3   b1   c2
9. a3   b2   c1
10. a2   b3   c1

How you rate . . .

10-16 Fair. You and your classmates are all going through lots of changes now. That makes it hard to keep on top of your own feelings and motivations, let alone figure out what's going on inside other people! You can develop your EQ by allowing yourself some quiet time to listen to your intuition. Spend some time, too, observing others carefully. You can learn a lot about what's going on inside other people by watching their facial expressions and body language. Before long, you will be a wiz at understanding yourself and others!

17-23 Good. You have a solid understanding of what makes you tick and what gets under your skin. You have good self-control too, and you don't let yourself fly off the handle or sink into a funk at every little thing. You also are pretty good at reading other people and can behave in ways that help you all get along. Continue developing your EQ to build even better friendships and healthier self-awareness.

24-30 Excellent. You are a pro at understanding human nature and human behaviour. You have a high degree of self-knowledge, and that gives you plenty of self-confidence. Others respect you, and you, in turn, respect them — perhaps because you recognize their feelings and respond sensitively and appropriately? Remember that your classmates may not all be as emotionally intelligent as you are — don't forget to cut them some slack. They'll appreciate learning from your wise and caring example.

Look for these other great quiz books!

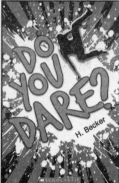